MAKE YOUR OWN
HORROR MOVIE

by Jonathan Quijano

Consultant:
Tad Kershner
Founder
Montalto Visual

CAPSTONE PRESS
a capstone imprint

Velocity is published by Capstone Press,
1710 Roe Crest Drive, North Mankato, Minnesota 56003.
www.capstonepub.com

Books published by Capstone Press are manufactured with paper
containing at least 10 percent post-consumer waste.

Library of Congress Cataloging-in-Publication Data
Quijano, Jonathan.
 Make your own horror movie / by Jonathan Quijano.
  p. cm. — (Velocity: make your movie)
 Summary: "Provides instructions for how to make your own horror movie"—Provided
by publisher.
 Includes bibliographical references and index.
 Includes webliography.
 ISBN 978-1-4296-7528-4 (library binding)
 1. Horror films—Production and direction—Juvenile literature. I. Title.
 PN1995.9.H6Q55 2012
 791.43'6164—dc23

                              2011029184

Editorial Credits
Editor: Lisa Owings   Media Researcher: Lisa Owings
Designer: Emily Love   Editorial Director: Patricia Stockland

Photo Credits
Rick Orndorf, cover (foreground), 13, 22 (top left, middle left, bottom left), 23, 24, 25
(bottom), 26, 28, 29 (top, middle, bottom), 30 (top, bottom), 31, 35, 36, 40, 41, 42, 45;
Pawel Gaul/iStockphoto, cover (background); Paramount Pictures/Photofest, 5 (top), 25
(top), 27; Universal Pictures/Photofest, 5 (bottom), 7, 19 (middle); Columbia Pictures/
Photofest, 6 (top); MGM/UA/Photofest, 6 (bottom); Monkey Business Images/Dreamstime,
8; Lane Erickson/Bigstock, 10; Suzanne Tucker/Shutterstock Images, 11 (top); Yury Zap/
Bigstock, 11 (bottom); Warner Bros./Photofest, 12, 19 (bottom), 22 (bottom right); Jon
Quijano/ Red Line Editorial, 14; Michal Bednarek/Bigstock, 17; Fred Goldstein/Bigstock,
18; MGM/Photofest, 19 (top); Red Line Editorial, 20, 39; Sergey Mironov/Shutterstock
Images, 21; Tereshchenko Dmitry/Shutterstock Images, 32; Andreas Gradin/Bigstock,
33; Arthur Kwiatkowski/iStockphoto, 34; George Mayer/Bigstock, 37 (bottom middle);
Shutterstock Images, 37 (bottom left); Olivier Le Queinec/Bigstock, 38; Karin Hildebrand
Lau/Shutterstock Images, 44

Printed in the United States of America in Stevens Point, Wisconsin.
102011   006404WZS12

TABLE OF CONTENTS

INTRODUCTION TO HORROR FILMS 4

ACT 1
BEFORE THE SHOOT 8

ACT 2
LIGHTS, CAMERA, ACTION! 18

ACT 3
AFTER THE SHOOT 40

EPILOGUE
YOUR PREMIERE 44

GLOSSARY 46
READ MORE 47
INTERNET SITES 47
INDEX 48

INTRODUCTION TO HORROR FILMS

Scary movies have always attracted tons of fans. Classic horror movies such as *Nosferatu* (1922) and *Bride of Frankenstein* (1935) were some of the first to quench audiences' thirst for thrills and terror. Today, movies like *Let Me In* (2010) and *Paranormal Activity* (2007) do the same.

Many professional filmmakers, including Steven Spielberg, started out making horror movies. Horror movies are exciting and cost little to make. Gory makeup and spooky lighting are all you need to create terror. The rest is up to your imagination.

HORROR GENRES

Different **genres** of horror movies have developed over time to appeal to every kind of horror fan. Each genre has its own set of **conventions**.

genre—a category of art characterized by similarities in form, style, or subject matter

convention—a style, technique, or other element that has become a tradition

THE SLASHER

Conventions:

- A slasher contains shocking murder scenes.
- The villain is mentally insane and wears a frightening disguise.
- The victims are usually beautiful females.

Examples: Alfred Hitchcock's *Psycho* **(1960), Sean S. Cunningham's** *Friday the 13th* **(1980), Wes Craven's** *A Nightmare on Elm Street* **(1984)**

THE MONSTER MOVIE

Conventions:

- The villain is a large killer animal.
- The monster attacks people, causing widespread panic.

Examples: Steven Spielberg's *Jaws* **(1975), Steven Spielberg's** *Jurassic Park* **(1993), Peter Jackson's** *King Kong* **(2005)**

THE ZOMBIE FLICK

Conventions:

- Zombies rise from the dead to feed on human flesh.
- People bitten by zombies become zombies themselves.
- Humans band together for survival.
- Zombie flicks contain scenes of exaggerated gore.

Examples: George A. Romero's *Night of the Living Dead* (1968), George A. Romero's *Dawn of the Dead* (1978), Robert Rodriguez's *Planet Terror* (2007)

THE SUPERNATURAL

Conventions:

- Houses are haunted by ghosts.
- Victims are **possessed** by demons.
- **Supernatural** films often have religious themes.
- They contain spooky sound effects and visual effects.

Examples: Tobe Hooper's *Poltergeist* (1982), Gore Verbinski's *The Ring* (2002), Oren Peli's *Paranormal Activity* (2007)

VAMPIRES/ WEREWOLVES

Conventions:

- Vampires lure victims with charm.

- Vampires suck blood from victims' necks with fangs.

- Werewolves are wild. They kill by brute force.

- Werewolves change form during full moons.

- Both creatures prowl for victims at night.

Examples: George Waggner's *The Wolf Man* (1941), Catherine Hardwicke's *Twilight* (2008), Matt Reeves' *Let Me In* (2010)

Fans continue to watch their favorite horror genres. They are eager to see these conventions used in new ways.

possessed—under the control of a powerful force

supernatural—something that cannot be given an ordinary explanation

ACT 1:
BEFORE THE SHOOT

Moviemaking begins with preproduction. As the film's director, you will have a lot of planning and preparation to do before you begin shooting.

CREATING YOUR PLOT

Every great horror film starts with a wicked-scary story. If you don't already have a plot in mind, here are some ideas:

- Base your plot on a nightmare you've had.

- Think of a real-life scary event and exaggerate it. Read the news for stories about break-ins, chemical spills, or new viruses.

- Use a scary experience from your past. Have you ever been convinced that someone—or something—was following you?

- Start with a classic horror story and give it a new twist.

THREE-ACT STRUCTURE

Like all stories, horror stories need three main parts: a beginning, a middle, and an end. In movies and plays, these parts are called acts.

ACT 1
- **Suspenseful** opening scenes lead the main character to encounter a threat.
- The main character decides how to deal with this threat.

ACT 2
- The main character acts on his or her decision, but meets obstacles.
- The main character realizes how to defeat the threat.

ACT 3
- The story comes to its **climax**.
- The main character defeats—or is defeated by—the threat.

suspenseful—creating a feeling of uncertainty about what will happen next

climax—the most exciting or important part of a story

THE SETTING

Where will your horror story take place? Think of spooky places that are available to you. You can make any location seem spooky with the right sound effects and lighting.

Shoot outdoors in a cornfield, wooded area, or cemetery.

Shoot in your basement, garage, tool shed, or attic.

You can even use your backyard. Shoot at night. Disguise objects you don't want in your shot, such as fences and furniture, with black sheets or other props.

TIP

A common strategy in filmmaking is to use what you own. That is, do not write a scene in a spooky castle if you don't have access to a spooky castle. But it can also be fun and rewarding to make it *look* like your scene was shot in a spooky castle. If you can think of how to pull it off, go for it!

THE CAST

Now that you have your plot and setting, you need a cast of characters to bring your horror movie to life.

THE VILLAIN

Horror movie villains create the fear that fuels the story. They represent common fears. The shark in *Jaws* played on fears about shark attacks. The ghost in *Poltergeist* played on fears about haunted houses. What about your villain will inspire fear?

Every villain has a weakness:

- Most zombies can't live if their brains get smashed.
- Werewolves are usually helpless against silver bullets.
- Vampires are often no match for sunlight or wooden stakes.

Freddy Krueger, *A Nightmare on Elm Street* (2010)

To make your horror movie truly your own, come up with a weakness that goes against convention.

TIP

Horror movie heroes often survive because they discover the villain's weakness.

THE HERO

Horror movie heroes represent hope. Heroes usually survive because they are unique in some way. They could be intelligent, courageous, or have special training. Maybe they are just lucky!

SUPPORTING CHARACTERS

Give your hero friends and other characters to interact with. This lets the audience see the story from different points of view. For example, a supporting character might disagree with the hero about how to deal with the villain.

Supporting characters are the most common victims in horror movies. Their downfalls create terror and suspense. The audience wonders, *will the hero meet a similar end*?

FINDING CAST AND CREW

You will need actors to play the characters in your movie. Ask your friends and family members for help. If they can't act, let them help you on set as part of your crew.

You could also hold auditions at school or at your home. You could even play a few roles yourself!

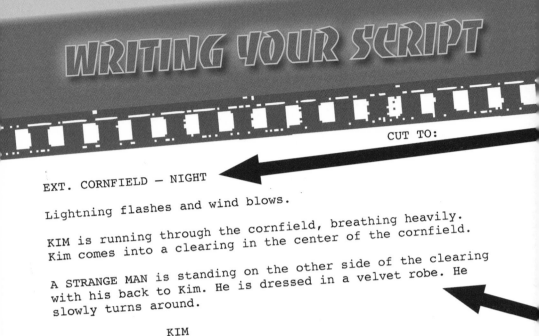

CUT TO:

EXT. CORNFIELD — NIGHT

Lightning flashes and wind blows.

KIM is running through the cornfield, breathing heavily.
Kim comes into a clearing in the center of the cornfield.

A STRANGE MAN is standing on the other side of the clearing
with his back to Kim. He is dressed in a velvet robe. He
slowly turns around.

                    KIM
              Who are you?

The strange man smiles, showing long fangs.

                    STRANGE MAN
              I think you know who I am, Kim.

Once you have your story, setting, and characters
developed, it's time to write your script. The script will
contain all the dialogue and action that takes place in
your movie.

Before you start writing, think about how long you want
your movie to be. Making movies always takes longer than
you think! Try filming a five-minute scene to get a feel for
how much time and work it will take to film your movie.

Movie scripts use a standard format, shown above.
The standard font is 12-point Courier. A film industry rule
of thumb is that in this format, each page of your script will
equal about one minute of film.

HEADINGS

- Start each scene with a heading that includes the place and time in which the scene is set. Use *DAY* for daytime scenes and *NIGHT* for evening and nighttime scenes. Use INT. (interior) or EXT. (exterior) to show whether the scene takes place indoors or outside. Make a new heading each time you move to a different place.

DESCRIPTION

- Describe the action throughout the scene. What are the characters doing?
- Describe the sights and sounds in each scene. What are the characters seeing, hearing, and reacting to?

DIALOGUE

- Write the speaker's name in capital letters above each character's line.
- Write your characters' dialogue. It is usually best to let your actors decide how to deliver their lines. However, you can include instructions in parentheses if needed.

script—the written text of a movie

dialogue—a conversation between two or more characters

PREPARING FOR YOUR SHOOT

Your shoot will go more smoothly if you take the time to get organized and prepare. But remember that no matter how prepared you are, things won't always go according to plan.

BREAKING DOWN YOUR SCRIPT

Most movies are shot out of order. All scenes that take place in the same location are shot at once. To stay organized, do what professional filmmakers do and break down your script. Go through your completed script. Make a list of where and when each scene needs to be shot. Also list the characters and props you need for each scene. Group together all scenes that need to be shot in the same place and at the same time. Use your list to make a schedule for your shoot. If you need to shoot outside, have a backup plan in case of bad weather.

READ-THROUGHS AND REHEARSALS

It is important to organize a read-through. In a read-through, you meet with the actors and they read the script. This gives the actors a chance to see how their parts fit into the movie. The read-through is also a chance for you to plan how you will direct and film each scene.

Rehearsals are also helpful, especially for scenes with special **choreography**. Watch the actors from all sides as they rehearse their movements. Plan where to place the camera.

choreography—the creation and arrangement of a sequence of movements

LIGHTS, CAMERA, ACTION!

You will shoot all of the scenes for your movie during production. It may take several weeks to shoot your horror movie.

CINEMATOGRAPHY AND EXPRESSIONISM

Horror filmmakers use cinematography to create a spooky atmosphere. Cinematography is the art of movie photography. It includes how shots and scenes are put together, camera angle and placement, lighting, and **special effects**.

The cinematography in many horror movies is inspired by a visual style called Expressionism. Expressionism started in painting, but Germans adapted it to movies in the 1920s.

special effect—a visual trick used in a movie when normal techniques won't work

Extreme camera angles
and shadows show
madness and fright.

Example: Robert Wise's
The Haunting **(1963)**

Actors use makeup and
exaggerated movement
to cause fear.

Example: James Whale's
Frankenstein **(1931)**

The setting reflects the
villain's evil nature or the
hero's feeling of terror.

Example: Stanley Kubrick's
The Shining **(1980)**

LIGHTS

Have you ever told ghost stories around a campfire? Maybe you tried shining a flashlight under your face to spook your audience. Horror movies use stage lights instead of flashlights to get a similar effect. Classic Hollywood lighting uses three lights:

1. THE KEY LIGHT

The key light is the main light on your subject. It is the brightest light, and it casts the darkest shadows.

2. THE FILL LIGHT

The fill light is a secondary light. It lightens the shadows created by the key light.

3. THE BACK LIGHT

The back light shines from behind your subject. It helps set your actor apart from the background.

Back Light

Actor

Key Light

Camera

Fill Light

There are no strict rules for lighting your scene. Experiment with different lighting setups until you get the effect you want.

Stage lights get hot quickly. Wear thick cloth or leather gloves when handling them. Plastic or rubber gloves can melt.

TIPS TO TRY:

- Use only a back light. Cast your villain in a menacing silhouette.

- Shoot without a fill light. The darker shadows create a chilling effect.

- Use no extra lights. Just a character holding a lantern or flashlight in the dark is terrifying.

FINDING LIGHTS TO USE

Stage lights are available for rent. You can also try using the lamps in your house. House lamps with swivel necks are best because you can aim the light. However, light from house lamps may make your shots look too yellow. Use your camera's manual to find out how to adjust the white balance. You can also replace the bulbs with daylight bulbs.

LIGHTING TO CREATE ILLUSION

Lighting can help your audience believe what they see is real. In normal light, your villain's costume may look fake. The right lighting can make it look terrifying. You can also experiment with **gels** for a more dramatic effect.

SHADOW SHOTS

Shadows hide part of the action. This forces the audience to use their imaginations to fill in the blanks. What they imagine is often far scarier than what is really there.

William Friedkin's *The Exorcist* (1973)

TIP

Lighting can affect the color of fake blood. Shoot test shots of your fake blood under different lighting setups.

Use a spotlight to show just the shadows of characters.

1. Place the spotlight on the floor. Point it at a distant wall.

2. Place the actors between the spotlight and the wall.

3. Film the wall displaying the actors' shadows.

gel—a thin, colored, transparent sheet used over a light to color it

23

CAMERA

The camera is the key to making a scary movie. You can terrify your audience just by clever camerawork.

USEFUL SHOTS

Try using these common horror movie shots in your own movie.

FINDING A CAMERA

The easiest camera to find might be a family video camera. You can also rent a higher-quality video camera. Even the video camera on your point-and-shoot camera or cell phone would work. It's not the kind of camera that's important. It's all about your creativity in using it!

DRAMATIC ANGLE:

A striking camera angle can startle your audience. Use shots from high angles, low angles, or canted angles.

CLOSE-UP

Use close-ups to heighten a terrifying moment.

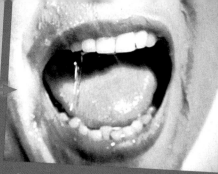

POINT OF VIEW (POV)

A POV shot looks through the eyes of a character. It can be a shot of the villain from the victim's POV or a shot of the victim from the villain's POV.

shower scene from *Psycho*

HOLD IT

Handheld cameras are often used for POV shots. The jarring movement of a handheld camera can add a sense of chaos to your horror scenes.

Examples: *The Blair Witch Project* (1999), *Cloverfield* (2008)

SURPRISE FROM BEHIND

The "surprise" shot is a horror movie staple.

1. The hero backs up, looking toward where he or she thinks the threat is coming from.
2. The hero spins around, only to come face to face with a frightening surprise.

canted—tilted to the right or left

25

The director guides the shooting of each scene. First, decide how to light and film the scene. Then help your actors give their best performances.

WORKING WITH ACTORS

- Give actors a chance to try the scene their way.
- Give your actors positive feedback after each take, or each time filming the scene.
- Frame any negative feedback as polite suggestions.

CHOREOGRAPHING A VIOLENT SCENE

In a violent scene, rehearsing choreography is essential. Both cast and crew need to know exactly what movements to make. Rehearsing also reduces the risk of injury.

Use creative cinematography to make your audience think they saw something they didn't. For example, if your audience hears a scream and sees a close-up of blood dripping down a wall, they will understand that a violent attack occurred.

STORYBOARDING

Storyboard each scene before shooting. Make a sketch of each planned shot.

storyboard for *Psycho* shower scene

SHOOT FOR EDITING

Be sure you film enough footage to edit later. Focus on getting the following shots for each scene. Film multiple takes until you have all the shots you need. Later, you'll edit these shots into a single scene.

ESTABLISHING SHOT

An establishing shot shows the location of each scene.

MASTER SHOT

A master shot shows the actors performing the entire scene. The master shot is the foundation of your scene. You can always cut back to it if you have a gap between your detail shots.

MEDIUM SHOTS AND CLOSE-UPS

Get a variety of shots of all your actors during each scene. A close-up highlights a specific detail in a scene.

Medium Shot (MS): shows the actor from above the knee

Close-Up (CU): shows the actor's head and shoulders

Extreme Close-Up (XCU): shows only the actor's face or part of the face

REACTION SHOTS

Show each actor's response to other actors or events.

INSERT SHOTS

Get close-ups of haunting details in the scene, such as a fire flickering in a fireplace or a door creaking open. An insert shot can also focus on an object that will become important later on.

SPECIAL EFFECTS

Pay close attention to how other horror movies use special effects to create terror. Any gory scene involves the use of special effects. Here are a few easy tricks you can try.

MAKE FAKE BLOOD

You will need:

½ cup (120 mL) water

1 tablespoon (15 mL) cocoa powder

¼ cup (60 mL) corn syrup

2 drops green food coloring

1 teaspoon (5 mL) red food coloring

1. Mix the water and the cocoa powder. Cocoa powder makes the blood look thick and dark.
2. Add the corn syrup and red food coloring.
3. Add the green food coloring to keep the blood from looking too red. If it is too red, it will look fake.

Fake blood is messy! Protect clothing and surfaces you don't want to get stained.

MAKE ZOMBIE MAKEUP

You will need:

liquid latex
(available at
costume shops)

cosmetic brush
or sponge

greasepaint in red,
green, black, and
a color slightly
paler than your
actor's skin

fake
blood

Optional:
- oatmeal or facial tissue
- black tooth enamel (available at costume shops)

1. Ask actors to puff out their cheeks. Then apply liquid latex to the cheeks with a brush or sponge. When the actors relax their cheeks, the latex will solidify into loose wrinkles.

2. Apply layers of latex to actors' faces and necks to create a facial texture that looks torn up. For added texture, stir oatmeal into the liquid latex before applying. You can also press facial tissue into the latex before it dries.

3. Use different colors of greasepaint to complete the look. Use a natural-looking pale color for the base. Add black paint under the eyes and beneath the cheekbones. Use red greasepaint and fake blood to create wounds. Green paint will look like rotting flesh.

4. Fake blood around the mouth is a must.

Optional: For extra gore, use black tooth enamel to create the appearance of rotting chompers.

GUSHING BLOOD

You will need:

fake blood

small ziplock bag

masking tape

1. Cut a small slit in the bag. Place a ½-inch (1.3-cm) strip of tape over the slit.

2. Carefully fill the bag with fake blood.

3. Use masking tape to attach the bag to your actor's skin, under the shirt.

4. When the actor is "attacked," the bag will break open, releasing the blood. The actor can grab the "wound" and force out more blood.

CUTTING EFFECT

You will need:

infant nasal
cleaning
bulb

fake
knife

superglue

fake
blood

straw

tape

1. Fill the bulb with fake blood.

2. Fit the straw onto the opening of the bulb. Use superglue to form a seal between the straw and bulb.

3. Hold the bulb against the fake knife. The knife should be facing the camera. Tape the straw to the back of the knife. The straw should reach to the end of the knife's blade.

4. Run the fake knife along the desired body part while squeezing the cleaning bulb. Blood will ooze from the straw. The knife will appear to leave a bloody trail on the skin.

ZOMBIE BITING INTO FLESH

You will need:

flesh-colored latex glove

cooked ground beef and spaghetti

fake blood

spirit gum (available at costume shops)

1. Fill the glove with a mixture of fake blood, ground beef, and spaghetti.

2. Apply spirit gum to the glove and to the actor's skin where he or she will be "bitten."

3. Let spirit gum dry until it becomes sticky.

4. Apply the glove to the actor's body where he or she will be "bitten." Disguise it with a loose-fitting shirt.

5. The zombie "bites" through the glove. It looks like the zombie is tearing into flesh.

MAKE STRONG WINDS

Use a leaf blower to create magical gusts of wind to accompany a supernatural event.

1. Stand offscreen, several feet away from the actor.

2. Start the leaf blower and point it at your actor.

3. Film the scene.

4. You can add whooshing sound effects later during editing.

MINIATURES

Not sure how to film your climax scene, where the haunted house burns down? It's easy to film a miniature house on fire. Ask an adult to help you set up and create the flaming scene outdoors. Be sure you are far from anything that could catch fire. Shoot the miniature straight on or from a low angle. This makes the miniature look life-size.

Check your local hobby shop for materials to build your miniature set. Look for miniature trees and other landscape pieces, model cars, and miniature houses. Use superglue to put your miniature scene together.

MAKE OBJECTS FLOAT

Use fishing line to make objects rise or float, a sure sign of a ghost's presence.

You will need:

screw-in hanging hook (available at hardware stores)

object you want to float

10 to 15 feet (3 to 4.6 m) of clear fishing line

1. Screw the hanging hook into the ceiling. Be sure to ask permission first.

2. Place the object directly below the hook.

3. Tie the fishing line to the object and run it up through the hook. The object needs to be secure so it will move smoothly through the air.

4. During the shot, pull the line slowly to lift the object. Be sure to stay out of the frame.

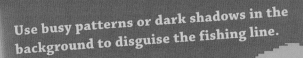

TIP
Use busy patterns or dark shadows in the background to disguise the fishing line.

ACT 3:
AFTER THE SHOOT

Congratulations! You've finished your shoot. Now it's time to edit your movie. This phase of the project is called postproduction.

FEAR-INDUCING EDITING

Editing is the process of **cutting** from shot to shot to build a **sequence**. Most computers come with a basic movie editing program. Here are a few tricks you can use in any editing program:

JUMP CUTS

A jump cut is a sudden, unexpected cut from one shot to another. Use jump cuts to make a scene feel frantic. For example, if a character is trapped in a room, you could use jump cuts to break up shots of your actor trying to pry open different windows.

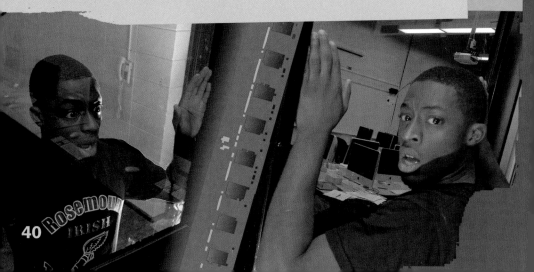

MAKE YOUR ACTOR DISAPPEAR

No film about the supernatural is complete without ghosts, ghouls, and other spooks disappearing before your eyes.

1. Put your camera on a tripod or other stable surface.

2. Film a shot of your actor. Film the same shot without your actor.

3. In editing, start with the shot of your actor. **Dissolve** to the shot without your actor. He or she will seem to vaporize!

TIP

If you reverse the shots, you can make your actor appear out of thin air.

cut—to change from one shot to another

sequence—a series of shots

dissolve—to fade one shot out as another fades in

SOUND EFFECTS

Sound effects can make an otherwise tame scene bone-chilling. Most sound effects are added to the movie during editing. These sound effects are called Foley. Sound effects are easy and fun to record yourself.

Punch

Whack a leather jacket with a baseball bat.

Slimy Creatures

Start with a gel-like food such as Jell-O. Stick a finger in it and stir it around. Get enough good sounds to edit into an overlapping collection.

Thump on Someone's Head

Drop a cantaloupe on a cement floor.

TIP Your movie set is a great place to record Foley. During shooting, make time to record echoing footsteps, creaking doors, demonic laughter, or whatever other creepy sounds you can dream up.

THE SCORE

Every horror movie needs a spooky **score** to heighten suspense and fear.

How to Make Your Score

♪ Ask a musically talented friend or family member if he or she will score your film.

♪ If you have musical training, try writing the score yourself. Watch your edited film and decide where to put music. Time how long the music needs to last in each spot, and write music to fit these spaces. Use microphones and sound recording software to record your score.

♪ If you can't get an original score, look online for royalty-free music, which you can use without paying fees.

Use your editing software to add your score. Now your movie should be complete! It takes just a few minutes to burn your movie to DVD after you save your file.

Two-Note Terror

The horror movie *Jaws* was about a bloodthirsty shark that attacked people. The movie was famous for the simple two-note theme that played whenever the shark was about to strike. When this theme started to play, the audience got scared because they knew what was about to happen. Try coming up with a musical theme for your villain.

score—the music accompanying a movie

43

EPILOGUE:
YOUR PREMIERE

At last, all your planning and hard work has paid off. Your movie is complete. Now it's time to give it a premiere!

Many small movie theaters let you rent their screens for showings. Your school or local library also might have an auditorium you can reserve.

HOW TO MAKE YOUR PREMIERE A SUCCESS

1. One month before the event, send invitations to friends, family, and everyone involved in the making of your film.

Include the following information:

- the name of your movie
- the date, time, and location of the premiere
- the length of the movie

TIP

You can have your premiere at home too! If you have a projector and projection screen, set them up in your living room. Otherwise, your TV or computer screen will work just fine.

2. Plan a short speech introducing your movie and thanking your team.

3. Serve refreshments and snacks after the movie. Set these up outside the theater or screening room, ready for when the audience exits. Bring music to play in the background while people mingle. Be prepared to answer questions about your movie.

4. Give your audience response cards to fill out. Ask them what they liked and didn't like about your movie. You may be able to use their feedback to improve films you make in the future.

Congratulations on making your own horror movie! Relax, and enjoy this feeling of accomplishment. You can start on your next movie tomorrow!

Give Your Premiere a Horror Theme

- Have your guests dress up in scary costumes.

- Make frightening decorations, or set up props from your movie. Spatter decorations with fake blood or red paint. Leave the lights low to keep the mood creepy.

- Serve spooky refreshments, such as blood-colored punch.

- Play eerie music that complements your movie. You could even play music from your score.

45

GLOSSARY

canted (KANT-uhd)—tilted to the right or left

choreography (kor-ee-AH-gruh-fee)—the creation and arrangement of a sequence of movements

climax (KLYE-maks)—the most exciting or important part of a story

convention (kuhn-VEN-shuhn)—a style, technique, or other element that has become a tradition

cut (KUHT)—to change from one shot to another

dialogue (DYE-uh-lawg)—a conversation between two or more characters

dissolve (di-ZAHLV)—to fade one shot out as another fades in

gel (JEL)—a thin, colored, transparent sheet used over a light to color it

genre (ZHAHN-ruh)—a category of art characterized by similarities in form, style, or subject matter

possessed (puh-ZEST)—under the control of a powerful force

score (SKOR)—the music accompanying a movie

script (SKRIPT)—the written text of a movie

sequence (SEE-kwuhns)—a series of shots

special effect (SPESH-uhl i-FEKT)—a visual trick used in a movie when normal techniques won't work

supernatural (soo-pur-NACH-ur-uhl)—something that cannot be given an ordinary explanation

suspenseful (suh-SPENS-ful)—creating a feeling of uncertainty about what will happen next

READ MORE

Draven, Danny. *The Filmmaker's Book of the Dead: How to Make Your Own Heart-Racing Horror Movie.* Amsterdam; Boston: Focal Press/ Elsevier, 2010.

Grabham, Tim, et. al. *Movie Maker.* Somerville, Mass.: Candlewick Press, 2010.

Lanier, Troy, and Clay Nichols. *Filmmaking for Teens: Pulling Off Your Shorts.* Studio City, Cal.: Michael Wiese Productions, 2010.

Rich, Susan, ed. *Half-Minute Horrors.* New York: Harper, 2009.

INTERNET SITES

FactHound offers a safe, fun way to find Internet sites related to this book. All of the sites on FactHound have been researched by our staff.

Here's all you do:

Visit *www.facthound.com*

Type in this code: 9781429675284

INDEX

casting, 13
characters, 12–13, 15
    supporting, 13
choreography, 17, 26
cinematography, 18–19, 26
crew, 13, 26

demons, 6, 43

editing, 37, 40–43
Expressionism, 18–19

filming, 14, 23, 26, 28–31, 38, 41
Foley, 42, 43

genres, 4–7
    monster movies, 5
    slashers, 5
    supernatural movies, 6
    vampire movies, 7
    werewolf movies, 7
    zombie flicks, 6
ghosts, 6, 12, 39, 41

heroes, 12, 13, 19, 25
Hitchcock, Alfred, 5

Kubrick, Stanley, 19

lighting, 4, 10, 18, 20–23, 26, 45

makeup, 4, 19, 33
music. *See* score

plot, 8
premiere, 44–45

read-throughs, 16
rehearsals, 17, 26
Romero, George A., 6

score, 43, 45
scripts, 14–15, 16
setting, 10–11, 16
sound effects, 6, 10, 37, 42–43
special effects, 18, 32–39
Spielberg, Steven, 4, 5
storyboarding, 27

three-act structure, 9

vampires, 7, 12
villains, 5, 12, 13, 19, 21, 22,
    25, 43

werewolves, 7, 12

zombies, 6, 12, 33, 36